SIMPLY SCIENCE

Electricity

by Darlene R. Stille

Content Advisers: Terrence E. Young Jr., M.Ed., M.L.S.,
Jefferson Parish (La.) Public Schools, and Janann Jenner, Ph.D.

Reading Adviser: Dr. Linda D. Labbo,
Department of Reading Education, College of Education,
The University of Georgia

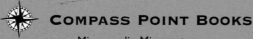

COMPASS POINT BOOKS
Minneapolis, Minnesota

Compass Point Books
3722 West 50th Street, #115
Minneapolis, MN 55410

Visit Compass Point Books on the Internet at *www.compasspointbooks.com* or e-mail your
request to *custserv@compasspointbooks.com*

Editors: E. Russell Primm, Emily J. Dolbear, and Melissa Stewart
Photo Researcher: Svetlana Zhurkina
Photo Selector: Matthew Eisentrager-Warner
Designer: Bradfordesign, Inc.

Library of Congress Cataloging-in-Publication Data

Stille, Darlene R.
  Electricity / by Darlene Stille.
    p. cm. — (Simply science)
  Includes bibliographical references and index.
  ISBN 0-7565-0089-3 (hardcover : lib. bdg.)
    1. Electricity—Juvenile literature. [1. Electricity.] I. Title. II. Simply science (Minneapolis, Minn.)
  QC527.2 .S75 2001
  537—dc21   00-010940

Table of Contents

Electricity in Your Life

What happens when you go into a dark room? You flick a switch, and a lamp turns on. The room is filled with light. What do you do when you want to watch your favorite TV program? You press a button, and the TV turns on. You see a picture and hear sound.

A switch turns on the electric lights.

A television needs electricity to work.

When you feel hungry, you could get a piece of fruit from the refrigerator. Or you might make some popcorn in the microwave oven. You can do all these things because of something called **electricity**. It is hard to imagine life without electricity.

A microwave is one of many machines in the kitchen that needs electricity.

Electrons are part of an atom. Atoms are too small to see.

Electricity comes from **electrons**.
Electrons are part of an **atom**. Atoms
are so small that you cannot see them.
You cannot see electricity either. But
you can see it at work. You see electric energy, and
you can see
electric
charge.

Benjamin Franklin and His Kite

Benjamin Franklin was a famous American. He lived in the 1700s. People did not know much about electricity then. Benjamin Franklin watched lightning in the sky. He thought that it looked like a giant spark. He wondered if lightning was electricity.

Benjamin Franklin ▶

◀ Lightning on a summer night

9

One day he tried to find out by flying a kite in a storm. He put a wire on a kite and tied a metal key to the kite string. Lightning hit the wire on the kite. An electric charge went down the wet string. The charge hit the key and made a spark. This told Benjamin Franklin that lightning was indeed electricity.

Do not try this experiment yourself. Lightning is very dangerous. Benjamin Franklin was lucky he was not killed.

Franklin used a kite and a key to prove that lightning was electricity. ▶

Making an Electric Charge

You can experiment with electricity yourself. But you can experiment in a much safer way than Benjamin Franklin. Get a balloon and fill it with air. Rub the balloon on the sleeve of your shirt.

Static electricity causes a balloon to stick to a surface.

The balloon will stick to your shirt. It will also stick to your hair or even to a wall.

What makes the balloon stick to things? Rubbing the balloon makes electrons move. Some electrons jumped from your shirt to the balloon. This gave your shirt and the balloon an electric charge.

There are two kinds of electric charge—positive charge and negative charge. Your shirt lost electrons. This gave your shirt a positive electric charge. The balloon gained electrons. This gave the balloon a negative charge.

Positive and negative electric charges pull toward one another. This is called **static electricity**.

Static electricity made the balloon stick to your shirt and your hair and the wall. Lightning is also caused by static electricity.

◀ Static electricity causes this child's hair to stand up.

Lightning is caused by static electricity. ▶

Electric Energy and Electric Current

In the 1700s and 1800s, people learned how to make a battery. A battery uses chemicals to make electric energy.

Scientists also learned how to build machines that make electric energy. These machines are called generators.

Today, generators in big power plants make electric energy. Power lines carry the electric energy to your home.

◄ *Batteries make electricity from chemicals.*

Modern electric generators ▶

Inventors found many ways to use electric energy. They invented the telegraph and telephone to send messages over wires. They invented **electric motors** to make machines run.

An inventor named Thomas Alva Edison invented the light bulb we use today. Other people invented radios, TVs, toasters, vacuum cleaners, and many other things that use electric energy.

Electric lights, TVs, computers, refrigerators, and microwave ovens all work because of **electric current**. Electric current is a stream of electrons that moves very fast. The electric current that you use in your house travels through metal wires.

Electric Circuits

Electric current moves in a **circuit**. A circuit is like a loop.

You can make an electric circuit with a battery, two wires, and a small light bulb. Your battery will give off electric energy. This starts the electric current. One wire carries electric current from the battery to the light bulb. The other wire carries current back to the battery. The light bulb uses the electric energy to light up.

Computers are run by electricity.

An early light bulb

Electric current flows as long as the loop that makes up a circuit is closed. A break in the circuit makes the current stop flowing. That is how you turn a light on or off with a switch.

Turning a switch off breaks, or opens, the circuit. The electric current stops flowing, and the light goes off. Turning a switch on closes the circuit and the electric current can flow again. The light goes on.

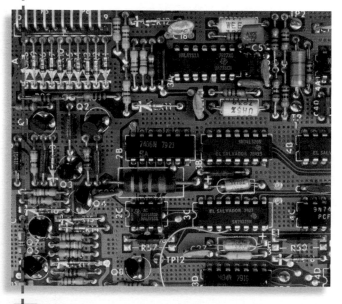

◀ *An electronic circuit board*

Many tools run on electricity. ▶

Electric Motors and Electronics

Electric motors use electric energy. **Electric motors** make many things work. Fans, blenders, power saws, hair dryers, and other things have electric motors. Electric energy makes the parts in a motor move. This makes the electric motor do its job.

Not everything that uses electric energy has a motor. Computers do not have motors. Radios and televisions do not have motors. These things have **electronic** parts. Electronic parts do not move.

◀ There is an electric motor inside this blender.

◀ A radio

Computers have tiny electronic circuits. Electronic circuits are printed on computer chips. Some chips are as small as your fingertip. Switches in the chip turn the electric current on and off. TVs, cars, and many other things have computer chips inside them too.

A computer chip

Computer chips are very tiny!

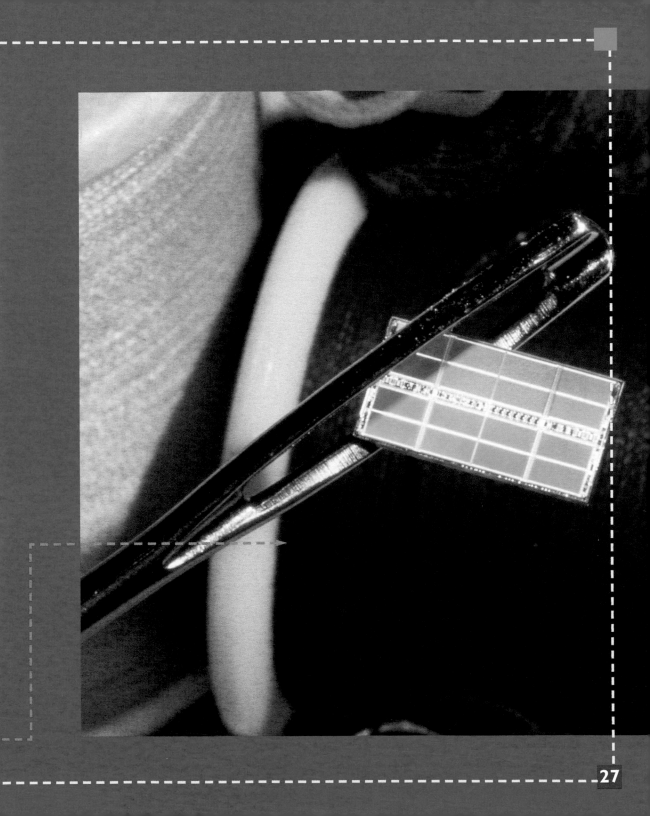

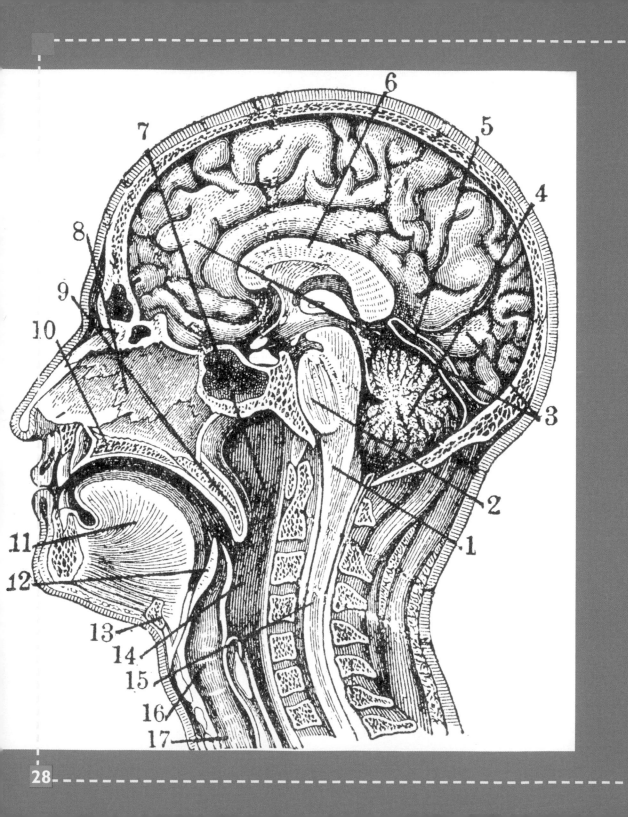

Electricity in Your Body

Your body uses electricity. Nerves carry messages to and from your brain. These messages are made up of electric signals. The signals tell your arms and legs to move. The signals tell your heart to beat. The signals also let you dream and think.

Electricity is everywhere. It is one of the most important things in our world.

The brain is the message center that controls electric signals sent throughout the body.

Glossary

atom—a tiny unit of matter. Everything in the world is made of atoms.

circuit—the path that carries an electric current from its source to the equipment that uses electricity to work

electric current—a stream of electrons that move very fast

electric motors—machines that use magnets to make energy run appliances and other equipment

electricity—a natural form of energy made by moving electrons.

electronic—using electric energy without having a motor. Computers and televisions are electronic.

electrons—one of the three particles that make up an atom. An electron has a negative electrical charge.

static electricity—a natural form of electricity produced by electrons as they move through air.

Did You Know?

- Benjamin Franklin's son, William, helped his father with his famous kite experiment. William ran back and forth until the kite was flying high in the air. Then he handed the kite string to his father.

- If lightning hits sand, it can make a hard rock called fulgurite.

- A nerve is made up of a bundle of nerve cells. Some nerves are up to 39 inches (100 centimeters) long.

Want to Know More?

At the Library

Cole, Joanna. *The Magic School Bus and the Electric Field Trip.* New York: Scholastic, 1999.

Evans, Neville. *The Science of a Light Bulb.* Austin, Tex.: Raintree Steck-Vaughn, 2000.

Riley, Peter D. *Electricity.* Danbury, Conn.: Franklin Watts, 1998.

On the Web

Being Safe around Electricity

http://www.tec-rec.com/kids/safety.html

For information about how to stay safe around electricity

Electricity Online

http://library.thinkquest.org/28032/cgi-bin/psparse.cgi?src=home

For information about the discovery of electricity and all the ways we use it

Through the Mail

Virginia Power

P.O. Box 26666

Richmond, VA 23261

To order a package with games and experiments as well as safety tips

On the Road

Boston Museum of Science

Science Park

Boston, MA 02114

617/723-2500

To visit the museum's Elihu Thomson Theater of Electricity, which has a two-story high voltage electricity generator

Index

About the Author

Darlene R. Stille is a science editor and writer. She has lived in Chicago, Illinois, all her life. When she was in high school, she fell in love with science. While attending the University of Illinois, she discovered that she also enjoyed writing. Today she feels fortunate to have a career that allows her to pursue both her interests. Darlene R. Stille has written more than thirty books for young people.